PIERO

DELLA FRANCESCA

THE AREZZO FRESCOES

First published in Great Britain in 1996 by
Thames and Hudson Ltd, London

© 1995 by Editions Assouline, Paris, 1995
Photography © by RMN, Paris, 1995

British Library Cataloguing-in-Publication Data

A catalogue record for this book is available from the British Library

ISBN 0-500-23718-2

Printed and bound in Italy

PIERO
DELLA FRANCESCA

THE AREZZO FRESCOES

TEXT BY MICHAEL MICHAEL

THAMES AND HUDSON

The Myth of Piero

E sebbene il tempo, il quale si dice padre della verità, o tardi o per tempo manifesta il vero; non e però che per qualche spazio di tempo non sia defraudato dell'onore che si dee alle fatiche colui che ha operato: come avvenne a Piero della Francesca dal Borgo S. Sepolcro ...

And although Time, which is called the father of Truth, sooner or later brings the truth to light, yet [many] are for some time defrauded of the honour due to their labours. This was the case with Piero della Francesca of Borgo San Sepolcro...

Giorgio Vasari, The Lives of the Painters, Sculptors and Architects, *1550 and 1568*

Vasari's opening remarks to his life of Piero della Francesca seem particularly apt. Piero's work was collected as an historical curiosity in the nineteenth century, and it was not until the twentieth century that the clear mathematical structure and balanced colour displayed in his painting was appreciated again. Perhaps this is because we are now conditioned to view the hidden structure and intellectual beauty of works by artists such as Poussin and Cézanne. Vasari saw Piero as an 'imitator of reality' and marvelled at his intellectual capabilities in having written mathematical treatises on geometry and perspective. In these books Piero appears to believe that the art of painting is so closely allied with the mathematics of perspective that the two

4

form one and the same discipline. The theosophical aspects of this unified view of painting as a process of discovery – finding the hidden structure in what appears to be reality – is usually viewed as an aspect of Piero's 'modernity'. Yet the meaning of Piero's art cannot be sought through just a formal analysis of the structure of his paintings. His work is often said to form a bridge between the fifteenth and the sixteenth century (certainly this is Vasari's view). But its timeless appeal suggests, paradoxically, that just the opposite is the case: Piero's approach to form and space enabled the traditional subject matter of his religious paintings to be expressed more forcefully. It makes a visual statement that leads neither forwards nor backwards because it seeks perfection.

Piero's painting almost single-handedly represents all those qualities which epitomize the Renaissance for us: use of linear perspective, visual references to Graeco-Roman architecture and sculpture and the humanistic concentration on individual identity and achievement. Yet the True Cross cycle in San Francesco at Arezzo is essentially a visual essay about belief and the power of unseen forces, which inexorably unravel over hundreds of years. The culture which lies behind the meaning of the frescoes is as old as the Legend of the True Cross itself, but the method of depiction is modern. The challenge for Piero was to make things more real in volume, space and colour, whilst developing a visual argument for the timeless and inevitable cycle of life and death that forms the narrative. The Arezzo cycle succeeds in making the unbelievable believable and tells a story in an untraditional way.

The Commission

Maestro Pietro di Benedetto dal Borgho Santo Sepolchro, Maestro di depingniere, el quale à dipinto la Chapela magiore di San Francesco d'Arezo...

Maestro Pietro di Benedetto dal Borgho Santo Sepolchro, he who painted the main chapel at S. Francesco in Arezzo...

Records of Compagnia dell' Annunziata, Arezzo, 1466

Piero was commissioned to paint the cappella maggiore of the church of San Francesco in Arezzo around 1452 by members of the Bacci family, merchants long associated with the patronage of the church. Franciscans had camped outside Arezzo as early as 1211, when Brother Silvester, a man of 'dovelike simplicity', was asked by St Francis (1181–1226) to go up to the city and expel demons who were causing civil unrest. St Francis himself received the stigmata at Mount La Verna (between Arezzo and Florence) when he was praying to St Michael on the feast of the Exaltation of the Holy Cross (14 September). Thus the significance of the Cross to the Franciscans, and its link to their preaching mission, would have been clear to all. The Legend of the True Cross had already been painted by Agnolo Gaddi in the cappella maggiore of Santa Croce, Florence (c. 1388–92). The influence of this cycle had spread to the Franciscan Church at Volterra (by Cenni di Francesco, c. 1410), and is seen in the Chapel of St Helena at St Stefano, Empoli (by Masolino, c. 1424). It must be in response to this that the Bacci and their Franciscan advisers chose this theme for their chapel.

P iero was born near Arezzo at Borgo San Sepolcro between 1414 and 1416, and had already qualified as a painter by December 1432, when he is described as 'pictor' assisting Master Antonio di Giovanni of Anghiari, to whom he was probably apprenticed. Piero was not the first choice for the commission. It had been given to the Florentine artist Bicci di Lorenzo, and in all probability the content of the cycle was already decided before his death in 1452. We do not know for sure when Piero started work, but it was certainly finished by 1466.

Piero had worked with Domenico Veneziano on a cycle of the life of the Virgin in the church of Sant' Egidio at the hospital of Santa Maria Nuova, Florence from 1439 (these no longer survive), and they later painted together in the sacristy of the church at Loreto until 1447. Much has been made of their association in an attempt to explain Piero's style of painting, but it is now certain that he was not apprenticed to him. His surviving mature work is almost entirely confined to commissions from the papal states and in particular princely and confraternal patrons. Nevertheless, he was always willing to take on commissions from his own locality, such as the famous *Madonna del Parto*, painted for his mother's home town of Monterchi, the *Baptism for the Priory of St John the Baptist* at Borgo San Sepolcro, the *Resurrection* for its town hall or the altarpiece for the confraternity of the Misericordia. The latter was commissioned in 1445, but Piero's work on it appears to have been so intermittent that he only received final payment in 1462, a clear indication of his peripatetic life at this time.

Reading the Cycle

Et imperò commo zelante de la gloria de l'arte et di questa età...

Because I am uncompromising about the glory of art in this age...

Piero della Francesca, De Prospectiva Pingendi, *c.1480.*

much has been written about the possible ways of reading the cycle of the True Cross at Arezzo; analogical, typological, liturgical and political symbolisms have all been detected, and very ingenious ways of constructing a 'narrative' have been suggested. Certainly, the text of Jacobus de Voragine's *Golden Legend* (c. 1250), which emphasizes the feasts of the Invention (3 May) and Exaltation (14 September) of the Holy Cross, lies behind the choice of scenes.

At the heart of the square cappella maggiore hung the great thirteenth-century Cross, with St Francis at the feet of Christ, brought by the community to Arezzo in 1290, before even the building of the church had begun (c. 1316–17), together with the bones of Beato Benedetto Sinigardi (d. 1282), its first guardiano. A companion of St Francis, Sinigardi, an Aretine noble, had spent many years preaching reconciliation to Christians and Saracens in

Antioch before returning to Arezzo in 1259. His sarcophagus was originally placed in a niche on the south side, which was filled in to facilitate the painting of the frescoes. These facts lie at the heart of the clear but crude message of redemption through the Cross chosen by the iconographer.

Piero has a painter's priorities, and it is these priorities which should also interest us. It is usual to describe the frescoes from top to bottom, as if looking at an architect's plan of the Salvation, but Piero's intention was surely the opposite, first capturing our attention at eye level on the 15-metre-high walls. On the north and south, at the lowest levels, above an imitation marble dado wall, Piero painted two most impressive battle scenes. The multiplicity of figures, the clash of colours and attention to detail all contribute to an inducement of awe. It is not often that one thinks of sound when looking at a picture, but the silence of the pictures is almost excruciating. Individuals open their mouths and scream without making a noise. The two scenes concentrate the eye in different ways. The *Victory of Constantine*, on the south wall, emphasizes a clearing in the centre of the composition as Constantine, dressed as a contemporary Byzantine emperor, marches steadily forward at a slow pace holding out a diminutive cross before him. This is the cross he had been told to take in his hand by God in order to defeat Maxentius, according to the *Golden Legend*'s reading for the feast of the Finding of the Holy Cross. A confused retreat on the left forms a compositional pyramid; its defining limits are the huge red banner and horse with collapsed rear quarters. On the right, a second banner and a group of lances, form an angle in the top right corner. The lances of the advancing forces lean slowly to the right, thus emphasizing an inexorable compositional movement from left to right. The vista in the centre forms almost a parallelogram. It is such a still scene that it creates a break in the cacophony around it.

On the opposite wall, the action is firmly placed in the centre. The forces of Heraclius and Chosroes are almost indistinguishable as the battle reaches a climax. This is the form of a medieval melee which was well known in manuscripts and in wall painting as early as the thirteenth century. It was a standard type of tournament combat similar to the Giostra del Saracino which still takes place at Arezzo, which Piero must have seen. Again the banners dominate the skyline, but they are carefully organized so that the baldacchino and empty throne of the captured Chosroes forms a continuity of forms against the skyline unifying the composition, whilst the scene of his capture and humiliation before execution forms a continuous narrative of the events of the day. It contains the variety of incident and contrast in composition that Piero must have intended, and which he certainly achieves. The defeat of Chosroes must also refer to the reading for the Exaltation of the Holy Cross, in which, according to the *Golden Legend*, Chosroes is offered his life if he accepts baptism, but he prefers death, and so is beheaded by Heraclius. Vasari's suggestion that portraits of the Bacci family were inserted into the group surrounding Chosroes is highly plausible – since, at this time, an increasing number of patrons were requiring artists to insert such likenesses into their work. But Chosroes' head is deliberately based on the cartoon of God's head in the Annunciation on the east wall – a clear reference to his desire to be called God the Father.

It is a relief to look up above the battle scenes at the central tier. On the south wall, a scene of courtly protocol is enacted with precision and clarity at a slow and dignified pace. Following the 3 May reading of the *Golden Legend*, the story of the Queen of Sheba's visit to Solomon is enacted. Sheba has arrived with a retinue of squires, who hold her horses on the left, and ladies in waiting, as befits a queen. She is shown kneeling before the wood from which the cross is to be made. It has been put to use as a temporary bridge across a shallow river.

t he action stops dead at this point as she venerates the wood. A large column, one of three seen in extreme foreshortening, divides the scene between this exterior space and the interior of a room where she is shown curtsying before the King. The figures alternate regularly by sex: male squires, the ladies in waiting and Sheba, male courtiers and Solomon and finally Sheba and her ladies again. Two trees dominate the skyline of the Adoration of the Wood, balancing the two groups of figures below, but the eye is drawn to the right by the curve of the ladies' trains and the downward thrust of the compositional pyramid which leads to the wood. The squareness of this scene is repeated in the interior, where the centrally positioned Solomon shakes the hand of Sheba. The figures are deliberately placed so as to emphasize Solomon and Sheba in the centre of a circle of figures: back three-quarter, profile and front three-quarter views are shown for both male and female.

Solomon is depicted in a frontal view, and Sheba in an appropriate left profile, to match her right profile at the Adoration of the Wood. That cartoons were reversed to facilitate this is clear – but it must have been done with a deliberate knowledge of the effect that would be achieved, and certainly not out of laziness. The choice of colours was also governed by compositional criteria that coincided with protocol. Bright reds and blues were used outside, but they were confined to the left hand group of men inside, with a small amount of red and blue to balance the composition amongst the women on the right. Nothing is allowed to detract from the brilliantly observed, but now badly damaged, white cloth of the gold mantle worn by Solomon. The typological meaning of these scenes – the prefiguration of the recognition of Christ by the Gentiles – often lauded as their true message, seems almost coincidental and a rather basic sort of intellectual assumption, beside the complex artistic priorities displayed here by Piero.

It comes as no surprise that the scene opposite should be visually paired with this. Again Piero has used an alternating scheme of male and female figures. At the extreme left ladies in waiting with St Helena, Constantine's mother, are shown where the crosses were buried by a group of men who retrieve them. On the right Helena and her ladies kneel before the Cross. It is laid on a dead man who rises from his bier, thus proving which of the three crosses belonged to Christ, whilst a group of men look on from the right. This scene has allowed Piero to show off more of his virtuosity in foreshortening, particularly of the crosses, but he has also given us a view of a walled city in the distance and a fine marble-faced temple. Just as before, back views, profiles and three-quarter views are shared out equally amongst men and women, with the leading woman depicted in profile, as if it were a contemporary profile portrait. But Piero has also taken great care to show different types of men, some with long beards, some with short, the old, the young – all demonstrating his acuity as an observer of life.

a gain the scenes are matched at the uppermost level. Landscapes, which allow the centre of the composition to fill the lunette to its peak with sky, open out the chapel. On the upper south wall, the dying Adam with his children allows Piero to show off his skills in depicting the extremes of old age by contrasting them with the beauty of youth. Eve is shown as a haggard old woman whose distended breasts are deliberately exposed. She is contrasted with a firm-bodied young woman wearing only an animal skin covering her breasts in the manner of an ancient Greek peplos, her long hair worn as a braid around her head. The dying Adam, seated naked on the ground, with only a small cape for covering, is similarly contrasted with an entirely naked young man seen from behind, leaning on a stick. In the background, Seth receives a branch of the Tree of Mercy from St Michael with which he hopes to cure his father. On the right, behind a tree which dominates the scene, Adam is buried as his children look on. Adolescent boys and girls, only partially clothed, are contrasted with mature men and women as the branch is placed in Adam's mouth; when the tree bears fruit then Seth's father will be made whole again.

On the north wall, the scene of the Return of the Holy Cross to Jerusalem by Heraclius gives Piero the chance to show off his intimate knowledge of contemporary Byzantine clothing. The elaborate hats of the two groups that confront each other emphasize the solemnity of the event. The action takes place outside the walls of the city and the Cross is displayed in a gap between two trees, thus elaborating its importance. The townspeople kneel before it, just as Helena and Sheba had done, but in this case they are all men.

Viewed from top to bottom, the scenes clearly relate to each other visually. On the south wall each register is divided into two main areas even if the space is unified: a scene on the left and a scene on the right. The dividing point is the tree, the column and the river. This division can also be detected on the upper two registers of the north wall, and even the Battle of Heraclius is divided into two scenes with the humiliated Chosroes on the far right, despite its centralized visual effect. All the scenes are enclosed on either side by inward-looking figures or compositional devices, which balance the action on either side. Thus, despite the logic of the arrival of the Queen of Sheba preceding her welcome as a narrative sequence, it is the balance between the two sides of the composition that is striking – and the same applies to the Discovery and Proving of the Cross depicted on the opposite wall. The continuous narrative that is presented is a visual whole with individual essays within it.

The east wall has been treated quite separately because of its relationship to the central crucifix, which once hung in the chapel. The Annunciation is shown on the north lower register, and we are invited to compare it with the Vision of Constantine on the south. The balance of male and female in the cycle would seem almost incomplete without this scene, for it is the Virgin who redeems the sin of Eve, and the two queens who are instrumental in the finding of the True Cross. The Virgin stands disproportionately tall beside a large column under a portico, not as an ordinary woman, and certainly not as a disingenuous young girl, but as the embodiment of the church: Ecclesia. It is as a symbol of victory that the angel carries the palm to her. She carries a small prayer book as she is the sedes sapientia (the seat of wisdom), but she can also be regarded as the Sponsa (Bride) of the Song of Solomon. Beato Benedetto Sinigardi had instigated particular devotions for the Feast of the Annunciation at Arezzo, but the clear typological significance of the scene when compared with the Vision of Constantine should not, however, be underestimated. If Piero did not choose the scenes he depicted – and there is every indication that he did not – it would be in keeping with the very basic typological message that the cycle displays.

the Vision of Constantine derives from the composition created by Agnolo Gaddi at Santa Croce, Florence, and used again by Masolino at Empoli. Artists were fond of this type of visual tribute, but Piero goes about his task with relish, using light and shade in extremes to depict a night scene with a deliberately reversed front and back view of two soldiers, and an incredibly foreshortened angel flying directly into the picture. Above this, he has depicted the scene of the Burial of the Cross and the Miracle of the Jew, who is starved by St Helena in a well before he tells of the whereabouts of the wood for the cross. At the very top, two prophets stand looking towards the centre of the chapel. When viewed frontally, these scenes frame the cross that hung in the chapel – the uprights on the left leading inwards, and the wood on the right angled towards the centre of the chapel.

t he accurate depiction of contemporary Byzantine clothing in the frescoes has led to the suggestion that some reference to the attempted reconciliation of the Eastern and Western Churches was intended. Piero must have seen Byzantine clothing at the Ecumenical Council of Florence in 1439, and Greeks were at the courts of Italy throughout the period, looking for support against the Turks. The fall of Constantinople in 1453, and the fear of Islam that spread in Western Europe, seems a particularly apt historical reference point for the frescoes, but Piero's intentions appear to be to give an accurate depiction of what he thought was 'Eastern Roman' attire. His combinations of modern and antique Roman armour and 'ancient' and contemporary Byzantine dress reveal his acute powers of observation in recording what people wore. That he links attire with religious, political and ethnic origins is not surprising. The general groupings that can be detected suggest that Graeco-Roman drapery derived from antique sculpture is associated with a far distant past. Byzantine dress identifies the Eastern Roman Empire (at all times), but contemporary dress is combined with this and fictive dress to suggest the class and function of people within the context of the story. Thus a fascinating historical mixture is presented.

Beyond the Myth

Colorare intendiamo dare i colori commo nelle cose se dimon-
strano, chiari et uscuri secondo che i lumi li devariano.

Colour we understand as giving colours as they are seen in things,
light and dark according to how light changes them.

Piero della Francesca, De Prospectiva Pingendi, *c. 1480*

the vast literature that has developed on Piero since
Kenneth Clark's pioneering book, *Piero della Francesca*
(London, 1951 and 1969) encompasses nearly every modern approach from technical reports to structuralist analysis. The
most reliable modern books are the first edition of Eugenio Battisti's
Piero della Francesca (Milan, 1971) and Ronald Lightbown's *Piero
della Francesca* (London, 1992). The chief contribution to our
understanding of Piero made by the recent literature concerns his
technique and use of colour, rather than the interpretation of
iconography. It is Clark who first mentions Piero's so-called 'dawn
lighting' and his complex use of colour. It should come as no surprise that he not only used the avant-garde science of perspective,
but also employed techniques for applying paint that stretch the
technology available to him to its limits. Piero's interest in the
effects of light and shade, and his desire to reproduce colours 'as
they are seen in things' (texture for some materials and luminosity
for others), must be what caused him to experiment in this way.
Paolo Bensi (*Atti del Convegno Internazionale*, Arezzo, 1990,
Venice, 1993) proposes that Piero's painting technique at Arezzo
indicates that he was in the vanguard of a technical revolution in

Italian fifteenth-century painting. But the variety of techniques used by Piero has caused a number of problems for the conservation of his paintings. The first modern restorations at Arezzo took place as early as 1858, and subsequent restorations from 1915 to 1916, and then between 1962 and 1964, under Leonetto Tintori, have struggled to consolidate what appears to be a technique of painting quite far removed from buon fresco.

S ince the current cleaning and consolidation was started in 1992 by the Opificio delle Pietre Dure, Florence, and the Soprintendenza ai BAAAS di Arezzo, headed by Anna-Maria Maetzke, it has become clear that Piero used both tempera and oil media on the wall, so that, for instance, some of the flags and banners are painted in pure oil technique and the river in the Victory of Constantine is painted using a mixture of azurite, white lead and oil tempera. The combination of these techniques with use of scale cartoons for the figures would suggest that Piero was trying to achieve a type of realism in his painting that combined form, proportion and colour through the use of the optimum technique for each.

Piero complains that 'those who have no knowledge of the potential of art' have mistakenly praised artists in the past. Clearly he treated his art as a serious scientific profession and did not suffer fools gladly. But he also knew what his patrons liked. When Giovanni Santi, Raphael's father, writing at the court of Urbino, compares Piero with his contemporaries, he states simply that Piero is 'antico più di quelli'. The antique qualities appreciated in his painting were, however, probably not merely the obvious ones which we all recognize in his classicizing architecture and figures, but much more subtle ones reflecting his ability to produce 'realistic' images. The humanist Bartolomeo Fazio praised this skill above all others, because it was admired by Pliny when writing on ancient painters, such as Appelles, Zeuxis and Aristomenes. Piero sought to be compared with and remembered alongside these artists in his own written works. He has surely finally succeeded.

Following page: *The thirteenth-century cross, attributed to an anonymous artist known as 'the master of San Francesco', currently in an adjacent chapel.*

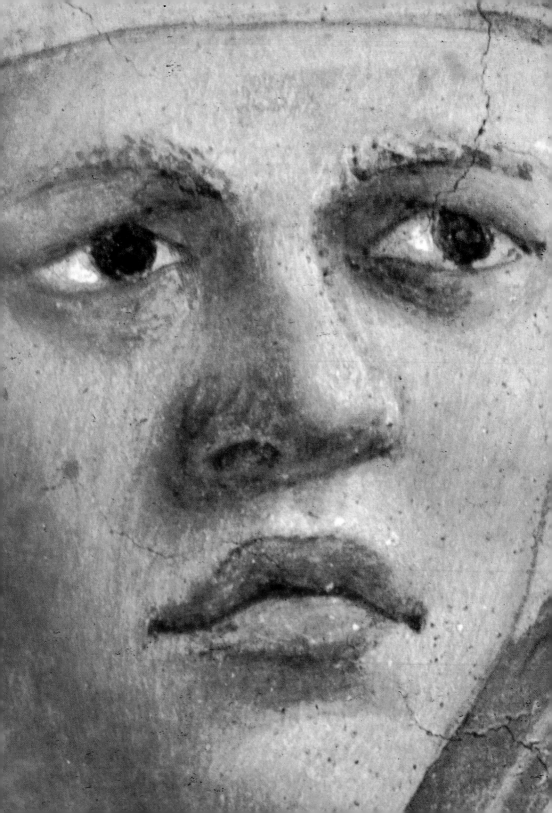

Frescoes in San Francesco, Arezzo

The Death and Burial of Adam
Adam's son Seth returns to the gate of the garden of Paradise and asks St Michael for oil from the Tree of Mercy to save his dying father. He gives Adam a branch from the Tree of Knowledge. When Seth returns, Adam is already dead, and so the branch is planted over his father's grave. The Tree flourishes until Solomon's time, when it is cut down for use in his new temple.

The Adoration of the Wood and Solomon and Sheba
The Queen of Sheba has come to test the legendary wisdom of Solomon. She refuses to walk on the wood of the tree, which was discarded because the planks intended for the Temple of Solomon magically kept changing size. She later writes to Solomon that 'upon this tree would one day be hanged the man whose death would put an end to the kingdom of the Jews.'

The Victory of Constantine over Maxentius
The reading for the Exaltation of the Cross says Constantine decreed a cross be carried in the vanguard of his army – but an alternate text says he took a golden cross in his hand as seen here. Later Byzantine emperors carried a relic of the true cross into battle. The composition is close to twelfth-century depictions, which may account for the choice of scene, rather than any textual source.

The Return of the True Cross to Jerusalem
The reading for the Exaltation of the True Cross recounts that the Emperor Heraclius, after recapturing the Cross from the Persians, carried it back to Jerusalem riding on a horse, but the gate was miraculously barred. An angel reminds him that Christ entered on a lowly ass. Heraclius removes his shoes and humbly carries it to the gate.

The Victory of Heraclius over Chosroes
According to the *Golden Legend*, the Persian King Chosroes captured Jerusalem in 615. He placed the True Cross at his side and a cockerel on the other, demanding that all salute him as God. He was defeated and beheaded by Heraclius when he would not convert.

The Discovery and Proving of the Cross
St Helena, the Mother of Constantine, is credited with the search that led to the Exaltation of the True Cross. The three crosses have been buried near a temple of Venus. In order to prove which of the three was Christ's, all are placed on the body of a dead man – only the True Cross has the power to bring him back to life.

The Cross
The thirteenth-century cross with St Francis at its foot hangs between the Annunciation to the Virgin, The Vision of Constantine (lower level), the Miracle of the Jew in the Well and the Burial of the Cross (upper level). When Solomon discovered the purpose of the wood, he had it buried. Helena discovers that one Jew, Judas, knows where it is buried. She has him starved down a well until he reveals where it is. The Annunciation can be seen as a prefiguration of the Vision of Constantine before the Battle with Maxentius. The Virgin is widely thought to have redeemed the sin of Eve, central to the story of the Fall and Redemption of Man through the True Cross. Constantine's dream is of a cross described in shining light with the motto 'In this sign thou shalt conquer'.

This book is dedicated
to the memory of
Andrew Martindale,
without whose teaching it
could not have been written.

I should also like to thank
Dr Jane Bridgeman
for invaluable help and advice
during the writing of this book,
and *Dr Paolo Bensi*
for information concerning
the restoration of the frescoes.